A CASE

— FOR —

WISDOM

Geoffrey Woods

humans and in its power to defeat evil. Evil, or that which is destructive, cannot manipulate wisdom since wisdom confronts the lies of evil by standing steadfastly in the truth. Wisdom never compromises the knowledge of truth, and evil cannot prevail against wisdom within this characteristic.

How does an individual find wisdom that is powerful enough to confront evil? What exactly is the process? In my experience I have found there are four steps:

- **A**cknowledge
- **S**earch
- **A**ct
- **R**econcile

The first letter of each word is in bold so you can easily recall these four steps with an acronym (ASAR). My book details each of these steps within the context of explaining my long, painful process of reconciling with my father.

I have left space in the book for the reader to answer questions. I hope you enjoy the process!

CHAPTER 1

ACKNOWLEDGING MY PROBLEMS

Acknowledge—the first step in gaining wisdom—stands for acknowledging problems. The desire for wisdom starts with the knowledge that there are problems in life that one does not know how to solve. I start my story with my childhood.

The Setting of My Childhood

I was born at Huntington Memorial Hospital in Pasadena, California, in 1960. I came home from the hospital to 2430 Cross Street in La Crescenta, California. La Crescenta, northwest of the hospital, would be my home for the next eighteen years. The one-story brick house had brown wood trim and hardwood floors. There was a big brick fireplace in the living room; down the hallway, off the living room, were three bedrooms and the "big bathroom." The "little bathroom" was off the kitchen next to the laundry room.

Due to an expanding family of two boys and then two girls, my parents added a large bedroom above the garage in the late 1960s, which my older brother and I shared. My paternal grandfather built a doghouse in the side yard. This was a great gift since we had several dogs. The biggest, a Saint Bernard named Danny, stood about as tall as I was at the time. The smallest dog we owned was a beagle named Buster. We always had at least one dog. If one dog died or ran away, it didn't take my dad much time to bring a new one home. My father loved dogs! His love for dogs was a point of contention between my parents; he loved dogs, but my mother didn't!

The front of our house was fairly large with a lawn and a driveway that led into the garage. A huge tree shaded a good portion of the small backyard so no grass would grow. My parents eventually built a deck in the backyard that we used during the summer. We always had enough room to play games among ourselves or with the neighborhood children.

Our street was one block above the main boulevard. The police station was on one end of Foothill Boulevard. Since the police station was located on Briggs Avenue, some people referred to the police as the "Briggs Pigs." There was an old stone Episcopal church where the neighborhood kids would ride bikes, play "Adam 12" or the "Mod Squad," make forts, and spy on people who lived across the street. That was the only church we attended as a family; I received my religious education there.

There were many two-parent families with children my age and older on our street. The fathers worked, and the mothers stayed home. My mother was a stay-at-home mom, and I always found it comforting to come home after school and have my mom there. We were free to play, ride bikes, and go to each other's homes since everyone knew each other.

We lived within walking distance of the elementary school, the junior high school, and the high school. I walked to and from school almost every day. It was a good school system, and I am grateful to my parents for providing a comfortable home, a good middle-class neighborhood, and good schools for my siblings and me.

Our life offered a great amount of potential for my family to be happy, but we didn't experience much happiness. We appeared happy to everyone in our neighborhood, and we kept up the appearance for a very long time. However, with time, unexpected tragedies and betrayals exposed the unhappiness.

The Fear of Death

When I was about seven years old, my father's father, the one who built our doghouse, was stricken with stomach cancer. My grandfather was a short, stout man. He played football in high school and, at one point in his life, he was a fireman—and he looked like both. Although I referred to him as Grandpa Woods, other people called him Stub. To this day, I still don't know why that was his nickname.

My grandfather was a strong, seemingly invincible man, but he eventually succumbed to cancer. I didn't see him while he was ill and didn't see my grandmother until his funeral. In the big black limousine, my brother, father, and grandmother sat directly across from me. I looked mostly at the floor because, every time I looked up, I saw my grandmother crying. She wore a hat, a formal dress, white gloves, and black shoes. I had never seen her dressed that way before, and I had never seen her cry so uncontrollably. I knew his death was a tragedy by witnessing my grandmother's grief, and I didn't like seeing her that way. I remained quiet because I didn't know what to do or say.

Several weeks after the funeral, I was eating my Wheaties or Fruit Loops at the kitchen table. My parents were talking about my grandfather. My father stood by the toaster, waiting for his toast. He explained how my grandfather's death had been horrific and awful. Toward the end of his life, he didn't even look like himself, and he suffered a great deal of pain. His cancer must have been a monster of a disease if it could destroy my grandfather and take his life. This disease must have been stronger than he was.

My naïve, frightened, seven-year-old brain tried to figure it all out. It was my first experience with death, and I thought about it constantly. I never wanted to get cancer, and I didn't want any of my family members to get it either, especially my mother or father. To protect everyone, I created a belief that cancer would attack only older people. I was certainly safe, and so were my parents. I was sure of this, and I was relieved! A great fear had been lifted from my shoulders because I believed wholeheartedly we were all safe from getting cancer.

Several years after my grandfather's death, my father's energy level started to change. He started to complain about being tired, but he blamed it on his new work schedule. He had started working nights instead of days, and he thought he hadn't adjusted to his new schedule. I convinced myself that he'd be back to normal in a couple of weeks with no problems, and there was nothing to worry about.

One afternoon, my brother and I were watching TV on the leather couch in the den. My father loved books and had built bookshelves for his hundreds of books. Our TV was in the middle of all the books. I definitely liked to watch TV more than reading books since it was easier to turn on the TV than to read!

While I was thinking about how much I preferred TV to books, my mother walked into the den. I was a little shocked because she was all dressed up, and she was so beautiful. She was slender with dark hair, and she was wearing a red dress, a dress that Jacqueline Kennedy would wear. As I was staring at her, she sat down in a chair across from us.

She said, "Your father has stomach cancer." She started to cry, and her crying turned into sobbing.

I sat on the couch, frozen as if I were watching my grandmother cry at my grandfather's funeral. *This can't be possible! My father's too young to get stomach cancer! He is much too young to get the same cancer my grandfather had. I can't believe this. Only old people get cancer! How can this be? How can this happen? If my father dies, what will happen to us?*

What will life be like without my father? Will my mom be able to take care of us?

I didn't want to face the answers to the questions that were spinning through my mind. I didn't want to face the possibility of my father's death.

My mom was crying uncontrollably. I didn't think she would be able to care for us if my father died. She told us he was going to have surgery.

When she left the room, my brother followed her. I was in shock. I couldn't move, and I didn't move for a long time. Finally, I walked to the kitchen and saw my brother.

"If Dad has surgery, will he be okay?" I asked.

7

"I don't know. Anytime someone has surgery, it's serious. They will have to cut him open, and that can be dangerous," he replied.

"He'll be all right. Won't he?"

"I really don't know."

In the weeks before my father's surgery, I tried hard to forget that he might die. I kept telling myself he would be okay. *He can't die and leave us. He's too young to die. We won't be able to survive without him.* However, the thought of his possible death was too strong for me to keep dormant. I tried my best not to think about it. I didn't want to think about it or talk about it with anyone.

My father asked me to go to the hospital with him.

"Why do you have to go to the hospital?" I asked.

"I have to have some tests done before my surgery. Will you please go with me?"

"Yes, I'll go with you," I said reluctantly.

Before his tests, we had lunch on an outside hospital patio. We were talking, and then there was a pause in the conversation.

My father said, "You know, Geoff, I might die."

I stared at him. I wanted to put my hands over my ears because I didn't want to hear what he had to say. I was so scared of those words. So many terrible questions raced through my mind while he was talking. I hated those questions! They tormented me. I lowered my head so I didn't have to make eye contact with him. I don't remember saying or doing anything else that day. I don't remember what we talked about or where we went afterward. I was paralyzed by the fear that I might lose my father. I might lose him to the same awful disease that had taken the life of my grandfather.

On the day of his surgery, I decided not to go to the hospital. I visited him in the hospital afterward with my mom and my older brother. The first time I saw him, he was on his right side with his back to us. I fixated on the many machines in the room. Tubes connected my father to the machines. When I saw my father with all these tubes taped to him, I noticed he wasn't moving.

Is he alive or dead?

I held my breath. I stared at him, squeezing my mom's hand and holding my breath. I waited to see if there was any movement from him. I was still holding my breath when I heard the nurse say to my mom, "He's doing just fine."

My father isn't dead!

I was relieved. I started to breathe normally again. When I walked around the other side of his bed, I was shocked at how different he looked. His face looked so much thinner, and his skin looked so pale. He didn't look like himself, especially with all the tubes.

The nurse looked at my mom with a smile and said, "He is recovering well from his surgery. He'll be able to go home in a couple of weeks."

When he finally came home, he was thin and weak. My father's cancer had moved from his stomach into his esophagus. They had removed part of his esophagus and two-thirds of his stomach. He had to learn how to eat again. If he ate too much—or ate food he shouldn't have—he would get sick and throw up. He also had to sleep elevated on a special pillow. If he fell off of it at night, he would start choking on the food that wasn't fully digested.

I woke up one night from hearing feet running on the hardwood floors. Someone was choking and throwing up. I sat up in bed in the dark, not knowing what to do. I didn't know what was happening.

My mom quickly opened my door and said, "Your cousin is coming over to stay with you."

"Why? What's wrong?" I asked.

"I have to take your father to the hospital," she replied as she shut my door.

He had fallen off his special pillow and was choking on the undigested food. He had suffered so much already, and health complications associated with his surgery and cancer continued. I began to hate this cancer for taking away the father I knew.

Sometimes, especially during the summer, he would walk around the house with his shirt off. His abdominal scar started low on his left side, moved across his abdomen, and continued all the way up toward his throat. I hated looking at that scar. It reminded me of the all-too-real possibility of his death; when I saw it, the nagging, terrible questions returned and my mind raced with fear.

My grandfather's death and my father's cancer created fear in me and my family. Now I know that if fear isn't confronted, it becomes an extremely heavy burden. It can corrupt people because it doesn't stay quiet or dormant. It grows and slowly passes through different stages until it turns into something dangerous and destructive.

Questions for the Reader:

1. What belief did I create for myself and why?
2. Did the belief I created do what I intended it to do? Did it protect me or my family members?
3. As a child, did you ever create a belief or beliefs to protect you or your loved ones from harm or danger? If so, take the time to write the belief or beliefs and whether they protected you from harm.

Fear Turns into Something Ugly

Things were definitely different after my father came home from the hospital. The whole dynamic of my family changed. The way we communicated with each other changed, and the way my father interacted with us changed considerably.

When he finally came home from the hospital, he wasn't the same person. He needed more rest, and my mom would often remind us that we had to be quiet so he could sleep. She also told us he wouldn't be able to do as much with us because he needed more rest. Therefore, he wasn't as involved with us as much as he had been.

The most noticeable change I noticed was my father's unpredictable behavior. I never knew how he was going to react to anything I might do or say. One morning, my mom had made us eggs. He was across from me at the kitchen table, and my mom was cleaning up by the kitchen sink.

"Go put your schoolbooks in the car," he said. He was going to drive me to school that morning.

"I'll put them in the car when we both have finished breakfast and are ready to go," I said.

"I told you to put them in the car!"

"I'll put them in the car when we're ready to leave."

"I said put them in the car right now!"

"No, it doesn't make sense. I'll put them in the car when we go."

"Damn it! I told you to put your books in the car. Put them in the car right now!"

"No."

"I told you to put them in the car. Put them in the car!" He started to pound the table. He kept yelling and pounding the table.

I stared at him. I didn't know what else to do. I could see the eggs on the side of his mouth that he hadn't swallowed because he was so busy yelling.

When he finally stopped yelling, he got up from the table and went to his bedroom.

"What was his problem? Why was he so angry?"

"I don't know. He was sure mad," replied my mom.

He drove me to school in complete silence. I didn't understand why he was so angry and irrational.

Another time, out of the blue, he came charging up the stairs into my bedroom where I was watching TV by myself.

"I can't believe you. You are just lying there doing nothing. I don't like it when you're like this. You should be reading or outside doing sports or helping your mother with the work around the house. You're just lying there. Get up and do something!"

I slowly turned my head behind me to see if maybe he was yelling at one of my brothers or sisters, but there was no one there. I had no idea why he was yelling at me. I wasn't teasing any of my siblings, and I wasn't causing any type of trouble. I didn't understand why he was yelling at me out of the blue. I stared at him and didn't say a word. When he was finished yelling at me, he left.

I was confused about why he was so angry at me. Since he came home from the hospital, he would be very quiet and aloof for a while and then, out of nowhere, he would start yelling. I didn't understand it, but it made me leery of him since he was so unpredictable. I didn't know if his yelling would turn into something physical.

Another incident occurred when my older brother and I were having a disagreement and he intervened.

"Please let me borrow this paper. I need it for a school project," I pleaded with my brother. My mother and father were also in the dining room.

"No."

"I need this. Let me borrow it!"

I got the same reply.

My father yelled, "Let your brother borrow the paper."

"No," said my brother.

Chaos erupted. My father started going after my brother. He was chasing him around the dining room table and he finally got a hold of him.

"Jim, Jim, let him go," pleaded my mother as she got in between them. She was trying desperately to free my brother from the hands of my father.

The next thing I saw was my mother on the floor. My brother ran out of the house, and my father chased after him. My father returned a few minutes later and said he hadn't caught him. My father didn't apologize to my mother, who was now standing up, and he went straight to their bedroom. I went to my room, crying and not understanding how asking for a piece of paper had turned into something so ugly. I had never seen my father push my mother like that. Something had changed, and something was wrong.

Similar scenes continued through the years. Home life was unpredictable and chaotic. There were momentarily times of laughter, joy, love, and caring, but the chaos created from my father's unpredictable behavior dominated my family life more than the good times. I also started to change from seeing and experiencing everything that had happened since my father's surgery. I started to make decisions based upon my fear of his death.

"You look exactly like your father," a relative said at a family gathering.

"No, I don't! People tell me I look like my mom's side of the family!" I replied.

I stomped away, thinking that if I looked like my father, I was going to get cancer. I was young, naïve, and fearful. I didn't want to get close to him because I thought I might even catch cancer from him like a common cold. I really didn't want to get close to him because I thought he might die. I intentionally drew away from him.

Cancer is a serious disease, and I had to be serious. What did I decide to do? I decided to become serious. I dropped my friends. I dropped out of sports. I isolated myself from others. Instead of playing sports and hanging out with friends, I studied. I came home from school and went straight to my room to study.

However, most of the time—even with my books open on my desk—I couldn't study. I couldn't concentrate because I would start thinking about my father's death. Thoughts about his death consumed me. I was much too young to be that consumed with death, and I became lonely. I was set in my daily, lonely routine just like the rest of my family. We did the same thing every day; the routine of our days was the same day in and day out. We clung to our routine for dear life as if it had the ability to save us from our problems—as if doing the same thing every single day would save us from the thought of our father's death.

Over time, the household atmosphere became negative, and the most visible sign of the negativity was teasing. Teasing became a routine in our daily lives. Siblings teased each other, parents teased children, and sometimes children teased parents. Our teasing wasn't jesting or just making fun of each other; it was often cruel.

Whenever I was frustrated, I would lash out and tease someone. The words I chose were negative; many attacked a person's character or a physical attribute. I was especially cruel to my sisters when they were maturing physically. I would make fun of their bodies. I do not want to write what I said because it was cruel and I'm embarrassed by what I said.

After I would tease someone or someone would tease me, we would say we were just kidding, or it was a joke, or the other person was being too sensitive. That wasn't the case. Teasing was a way to express my fear, loneliness, and isolation. It wasn't the right way, but it was a way of releasing the pressure and burden of the fear of my father's possible death.

One good thing that happened to me occurred outside the home. I became a Christian in elementary school at a Baptist camp I attended with a friend. We had stopped going to church as a family for a few years. I started going to another church on my own in high school, and I heard about God's love for us, how we are to love each other as well, and how we should forgive each other. I also heard about principles to live by, such as the Ten Commandments.

Fear of my father's death didn't remain dormant; it turned into distance, isolation, negativity, and anger. For me, it turned into hate. I hated my family life. I hated the distance between my father and me. I hated the fear of my father's death. I hated his angry outbursts. I especially hated my father's cancer for causing all of this. I was excited to leave this situation and move away on my own for college. I would be moving to a new place, a new start, and a new experience where I could leave all these problems behind me. I couldn't wait to leave!

Questions for the Reader:

1. What was a sign of negativity within me?
2. What did the fear of my father's death turn into? Consider my family as well.
3. Can you relate to this experience? If so, write it down.

An Affair

A few weeks before college, I was feeling excited and nervous. I was rummaging through the house for things to take with me. As I passed by the kitchen window, I noticed something strange.

One of our former neighbors, Mrs. Anselmo, was leaning against her car at the top of our driveway. I hadn't seen her in years. It was nice to see her talking to my mom. I noticed tears were streaming down their faces. I wondered what was wrong. When I realized I was staring at them, I walked back to my room.

When my mom came back inside, I said, "Mom, was that Mrs. Anselmo?"

"Yes. Yes, it was."

"I haven't seen her in a long time. How is she?"

"She's fine."

"Mom, why were the two of you crying?"

"Oh, it was something Mrs. Anselmo told me. It's nothing."

I thought it was strange, but I could tell by her tone of voice and the look on her face that she didn't want to talk about it. I didn't push.

"Come on, everyone. It's time for dinner," my mom called.

My mom had set the dining room table very nicely. It had been a long time since we had eaten dinner at the dining room table together. We all sat down to eat, but one person was missing.

"Where is Dad?" one of my siblings asked.

"I don't know. He'll be here shortly," my mom said.

We waited and waited for him, but he never came. We started dinner without him. I kept glancing at the empty seat at the front of the table and wondering where he was. After we finished eating, I went to my room.

After several hours, my mom called us to the living room. Everyone was there, including my dad. I was quite surprised and wondered why he hadn't joined us for dinner. The atmosphere was very serious. *What is going on?* I sat down to his right. My mother, brother, and sisters were seated to my right. It had been a long time since we were all in the same room.

"I have something important to tell all of you. It's going to change the life of our family forever," my dad said.

Oh no! His cancer is back. I had been waiting for that moment for many years. I knew it had finally happened. I knew he was going to tell us his cancer was back and he was going to die. My greatest fear was finally coming true! *I don't want to hear it. I really don't want to hear this! Please don't say it!*

"I'm in love with another woman, and I'm leaving your mother."

What? Did I hear him correctly? Did he say he is in love with another woman? His cancer isn't back? He's not going to die?

"This doesn't change my love for you children. I still love you. I don't love your mother anymore."

I couldn't believe he said that in front of my mother. I looked over at her, and she was sitting on the couch calmly with no emotion and no tears. The tears started flowing from the rest of us. After a few minutes, my siblings and I started to ask my dad questions.

"How long has this been going on?"

"For two years."

"Where did you meet her?"

"I met her at work."

"Where are you going to live?"

"I got an apartment close to work."

"What will happen to us?"

"You will stay here with your mother in this house. I will only be twenty minutes away."

My mother stood up and requested that we all hold hands and say a prayer.

"Heavenly Father, help us through this very hard time that we are now facing in our family. Give us strength to endure what lies ahead of us. Amen."

After the prayer, my father hugged us and said good-bye to everyone individually. I didn't want him to hug me! I was repulsed by what he had said. I didn't want to touch him, look him in the eye, or say good-bye.

Please don't hug me. Please don't come near me. I don't want to hug you. Please don't. Stay away from me.

When it was my turn for my dad to hug me, I complied even though I didn't want to. I hugged him and said good-bye. He grabbed some of his clothes and walked out the front door, leaving five people completely in shock.

We returned to the living room and sat down.

"I knew of the affair for two years," my brother said.

"How did you know?"

"One of my friends saw them together. He told me."

"Did you ever confront Dad?"

"No. I never did. I guess he has to do what he has to do."

"What does that mean?"

"He told me this morning," my mother blurted out.

"How did he tell you?"

"He came up to me in the kitchen and hugged me tight. He said that I was a very strong person. He kept repeating this, and then he said that he was in love with another woman and was leaving. And then he left for work."

"He just left for work?"

"Yes. I called him at work to make sure I had heard him correctly. It turns out I had. He asked me to tell you children, but I told him it was his responsibility to do that. I wasn't going to do that. We were to have our last dinner together as a family, and then he was to tell you. That didn't exactly happen, did it?"

"Is this what you and Mrs. Anselmo were crying about this morning?" I asked.

"Yes, it was."

"Why didn't you tell us then? How could you hold this in and keep it to yourself all day?" I asked.

"It was your father's responsibility to tell you. It wasn't mine," she said sternly.

We didn't sleep well that night, and it took a while for each of us to finally get to sleep.

After my father left, I wasn't sure if I should go away to college. However, after much thought, I decided to go. My mom completely agreed with my decision.

I didn't speak much to my father after he left; however, he did call me and I reluctantly agreed to talk. He came over to our house, and we sat out on the deck in our backyard.

"Are you excited to go to college?"

"Yes."

"Are you all packed?"

"Yes."

I was becoming uncomfortable and irritated with the small talk. We weren't talking about the real issue. When I grew tired of the conversation, I started to ask the important questions that had been on my mind since the day he had walked out the door.

"So who is this woman that you have fallen in love with?"

He was taken aback, but he finally answered the question.

"Well, she's married with four kids. She doesn't have many friends, she hates football, and she has a temper, but I love her."

"What? She's married and has four kids?"

I hadn't heard him say anything positive about her, but he said he was in love. *Am I missing something?*

"I can't believe she chose me. I know I'm not the best-looking guy in the world, and I'm certainly not the richest, so I can't believe she chose me, but she did!"

I became increasingly irritated with the words coming out of his mouth.

"Dad, I can't believe she is also married with four kids. You are committing adultery, and you raised us to believe that this is wrong."

"Don't I have a right to be happy? Am I not to be happy? I didn't look for this affair, but it just happened. I don't know how much longer I have to live, and I deserve to be happy. Look at everything I have gone through with my surgery. My cancer could come back, and I could die tomorrow."

I sunk in my chair. I decided not to ask him any more questions. I didn't want to hear about his disease, and I certainly didn't want to be subject to his anger. His surgery and the years since the surgery had been a huge struggle for him physically. We had all lived with the idea that he might die, and I knew this was a tremendous burden.

I agreed that he deserved to be happy, but I was confused because I knew adultery was wrong. After he left, I turned around and kicked the wall because I was so conflicted about his words and his justification for the affair. He said everything with such anger and emotion that I accepted his words. I guess I believed adultery was justified in this case, but I wasn't completely sure. There was one thing that was clear to me after this conversation: I was disgusted and angry with him. I was confused about why I was angry with him, but I was. I also made a decision that I never wanted to meet his mistress.

One afternoon when I happened to be home from college, the phone rang. I knew my mom was busy, and I ran to pick up the phone in her room.

"Hello. May I speak to your mother?" a strange woman's voice asked.

"Yes. May I ask who is calling?"

"Just tell her it's a friend."

"Mom, it's for you!" I shouted. I remained on the line because I sensed something was wrong.

"Hello," my mom said.

"Will you please stop asking your husband for money?"

"Who is this?"

"This is a friend of your husband's, and I am deeply concerned about him. Stop asking him for more money. He has enough pressure already."

I couldn't believe my ears, and I couldn't hold back.

"Who is this? Who do you think you are calling here and talking to my mom like this?"

"Geoff, this is your dad's mistress," said my mom.

"No, I'm not. I'm just a concerned friend of your father's. He is under enough pressure and doesn't need the extra pressure of giving your mom more money!"

My mom hung up the phone, but I continued speaking to his mistress.

"You're lying. You're the woman he left my mother for—aren't you?"

"No, again, I'm just a concerned friend, and—"

"You're a liar. You are his mistress. Let me tell you something. It is none of your business to call here and tell my mom what to do. Who do you think you are?"

"I'm very concerned about your father."

"If he has something to say to my mother, then he can tell her, but it isn't your business to tell her anything!"

"Look, your father is a very nice, good man, and he works hard. He loves you very much. He loves your brother and sisters as well, and—"

"If my father wants to tell me he loves me, then he can tell me—not you. It isn't any of your business. Let me tell you another thing: I don't like you, I never want to meet you, and I definitely don't want you as my stepmother! Good-bye," I said and then hung up the phone.

I was very close to cussing her out, but I didn't. I couldn't believe her audacity. I sat down on the bed to catch my breath. I was in shock. I couldn't believe what had happened! I had never met her, but I hated her. I hated her for intruding in our lives like that.

My mom was at the kitchen table with her head in her hands. She looked up at me when I walked in the room. She looked as if someone had kicked her in the stomach. I told her what I had said, and she put her head back in her hands. I hated seeing my mom that way! I went back to my room, hoping that would not happen again.

That was not the only time she called. Over time, the phone calls became more frequent and stranger. They were creating tension in our household. I decided to speak to my father the next time I saw him.

"Dad, your mistress keeps calling our house, and this is very upsetting to Mom. Will you tell her to stop calling?" I said one day when we were at lunch.

"I didn't know this was happening," he replied.

It was hard for me to believe he didn't know. "Well, now you know that she has been calling the house. She has been telling Mom what to do, and this isn't her place. She also has said things to me—and my sisters—that she has no right to say. Tell her to stop."

"Geoff, I don't have any control over what she does."

I sunk in my chair because I couldn't believe the words that came out of his mouth. He was unwilling to protect me, his own flesh and blood, from this woman. He had known me for eighteen years—and had only known her for two years—but he refused to protect me from her. I came to the conclusion that she must be more important to him than I was.

He drove me home from lunch. In the car, I wasn't paying attention to anything he was saying. I was staring out the window and couldn't wait to get out of that car and away from him. Finally, he turned into our driveway. I got out of the car, said good-bye, slammed the door, and went straight to my room.

Alone in my room, still angry and upset, I took a solemn oath to myself to hate my father and his mistress with every ounce of emotion I had. I committed myself to this! I wholeheartedly believed this type of hate would protect me from both of them—and would prevent them from hurting me.

A Confusing State

The phone woke me at eight o'clock on a Saturday morning. I hoped it wasn't him again. I really didn't want to speak with him.

"Hello."

"Hi, Geoff. This is Dad."

I felt a pain in my stomach. I leaned on the dresser in my dorm room for support. I was sleepy, but I knew the type of conversation I was about to have. Every time he called, I asked myself the same question: Why do I speak with him? My mom once said that he owed me for everything he put me through. I quickly came to the conclusion he owed me money. The money would help pay for some of my college expenses. I decided to speak with him every time he called, but I also decided I wouldn't elaborate in the conversation. That way, he would know I was upset with him, but I won't ignore him completely. When I asked for money, he'd give it to me!

"Good morning," I said with my eyes half-open and indifference in my voice.

"How's it going? How are your studies?"

"Fine."

Long pause.

"Are you having fun?"

"Yeah."

Silence.

"So what's new?"

"Nothing."

More painful silence.

"Okay. I will call you next week." He sounded upset.

"Bye."

I crawled back into bed and put the covers over me. I hoped that sleep would help me forget the painful conversations.

I also hoped he wouldn't call me the next week. I hated speaking with him! *Is the money I get from him worth the game I'm playing with him?*

I started to think the money wasn't worth it, but if he didn't owe me money, what did he owe me? I committed myself to hating him. *Should I speak to him even though I hate him?* My reasoning and commitments started to confuse me. I wasn't completely convinced they were right. Little did I know that more confusion would follow.

"Hello. Is this Geoff?"

"Yes, it is. Who is this?"

"This is Teri." It was my father's mistress.

"You are not to be calling here. There's a restraining order against you," I said immediately.

She had continued to call the house to speak with my mom and my sisters. The calls had become more frequent and more vulgar. In one of the last conversations she had with my younger sister, she told her that she had been sleeping with my father for over five years. However, she used a vulgar cuss word to describe having sex with my father. My sister at the time was thirteen; that was the main reason why my mother had a restraining order placed on her.

"Please don't spit on me like they did Jesus," she pleaded.

What does this mean? Is she crazy? My mind quickly went to thinking that I should be nice to her even though she wasn't nice to me or my family. *I'll be a good Christian and listen to her.*

"Okay. What do you want to say?"

She started talking, and I had no idea what she was saying. Her words didn't make any sense. I found out from my father she was an alcoholic, so I assumed she must have been drinking because she was slurring her words and was incoherent. I surmised from her crazy talk that her relationship with my father was over. I am not sure, but I think she was trying to find some type of solace from me. I was thankful when I heard her say good-bye.

Thank God that conversation is over! I was so mad at her and mad at myself for listening to her. Why would I listen to my father's mistress whom I vowed to hate? Was I the crazy one? I thought my commitment to hating her and my father would protect me from them. I thought it would give me the courage to stand up to them and not speak to them. Why didn't my belief in hating the two of them work? I was angry and confused. Was I hiding from something? I thought back to what people had said to me about my father and our family. I thought back to conversations with my mother, father, neighbors, and other relatives. I made a decision to analyze what I heard and what I accepted from these conversations.

"Your father is a good man," one of my aunts said at a family function where my father was also present.

Yes, I know he's my father, but is he a good man if he had an affair? Is he a good man if he won't protect us from his mistress? Is this true or was she saying this to offer me comfort in an uncomfortable situation?

I accepted the statement from my aunt because she was an adult, but this acceptance that my father was a good man left me confused.

"He's your father and he loves you," my mom said when I didn't want to see him. I didn't understand why she would say this since she didn't want to see him or talk to him. I was not convinced he loved me because of his past actions. The statement offered me confusion and not comfort.

"Everything is going to be okay. My divorce isn't as bad as other people's," my mother said when I was home from college.

Really? How many other people's divorces involved an affair with the mistress calling the house and telling the ex-wife and children what to do? How many divorces involved the drunken mistress calling and speaking inappropriately to the children? Also, the situation didn't even change with a restraining order. How is everything going to be okay?

I didn't know what to do with this statement because I didn't think things within our family were okay. I knew they were bad. I never expressed what I really thought because no one else was saying what I truly thought. I thought her statement was trite and she was trying to give me some type of false comfort. Again, I was confused.

"He's your father, and he owes you," my mother told me when I had asked her for money for college expenses. She told me to ask my father. I knew he's my father, but what exactly did he owe me for leaving the family and not protecting us from his mistress?

I accepted that what he owed me for cheating on my mother and leaving me was money. However, giving me money didn't change how I felt about him or help alleviate the pain from the situation. Over time, I became increasingly more reluctant to ask him for money. It just didn't seem right.

"Don't I have the right to be happy?" said my father to me during one of our previous conversations. He had the right to be happy, and he had suffered greatly, but what about the rest of us? Didn't all of us suffer in some way from his cancer? Obviously he suffered the most physically, but there was fear and pain on our part. We were wondering whether he was going to live or die, and because of these things, there was unhappiness and despair. When he brought up his cancer, I willfully submitted that he had the right to be happy more than the rest of us did. This didn't lead to more clarity or healing.

I also started to question if my dad really loved his kids. It seemed to me that he had abandoned us. He also didn't protect us from his mistress. How exactly did he love us? I quietly accepted what he said as the truth and never questioned him, but I wasn't convinced he really knew how to love us. I was confused by his words and actions because they didn't seem to match.

"Love just happens. I have no control over it," he said.

Is this true? No one has control over their feelings of love? Look at whom you were in love with! You were in love with a woman who was married and had children. She was an alcoholic, and she was mean and vulgar. Why can't you have control over whom you fall in love with?

If no one had control over love, I didn't want it. I made a commitment to myself never to get it. I thought there had to be a greater meaning to love than what I saw. I had no idea what it was, but there had to be!

"No one is ever truly happy." said my father. *Really? Out of all the people in the world, no one person is happy? No one person has found happiness? Is this true?*

I accepted his statement as true, even though I had questions about the validity of his statement. As a result of this acceptance, I never pursued happiness on a deep, mature level.

"I can't believe you think I hate your mother. I left because I fell out of love with her—not because I hated her," he said during one of our arguments. It sounded good, but it looked like he did hate her from the way he treated her. Was there no anger or resentment on his part toward my mother? Again, I accepted this statement even though I didn't believe it since he said it with so much anger and emotion. My passive acceptance left me even more confused about love and hate.

"There's a lot of love in your family," one of our neighbors said to my mother right after my father moved out.

Is there really a lot of love in our family? It sounds nice, but is it true? It seems there's more negativity, anger, lying, and cheating than love. Again, for me, there was more confusion about what love is.

All these examples show the confusion that was inside of me. Specifically, I was confused about what my father actually owed me from leaving the family, and I was also confused about love. I didn't understand what it was. I believed in God's love and knew that it was much greater than human love. I also knew from my teachings at church that we are to love one another. I didn't think the type of love in my family was the type of love God wants us to have for each other. *What type of love does God want us to show each other?* I didn't have any idea.

Several years passed before the principle of forgiveness emerged within my family, and it started with my mother and then my father.

One day, my mom told me she had forgiven my father for his affair. Once she had done this, she was able to talk with him. It was a relief to see them sit down and talk peacefully. Since she didn't tell him she forgave him, I wasn't sure this was true forgiveness as opposed to letting go of bitterness.

"I forgave your father—well, not really," my mother said many years later.

What did that mean? I had noticed that she was still angry about the divorce.

One evening, my father and my siblings were at the kitchen table like we had done when we were young.

"I am very sorry for my affair," my father blurted out.

Everyone was silent for a moment. I don't think anyone expected it at all, especially since we weren't talking about his affair or divorce.

"I think we all have forgiven you," said my sister.

"You know you caused a lot of pain?" I said to my dad.

He agreed. At that moment, I hadn't forgiven him. Those were easy words to say that didn't grasp the tremendous amount of pain he had caused. I thought there was something missing. He owed us something besides saying he was sorry.

As a Christian, I knew that we are to forgive one another, but the way my mom and dad forgave didn't seem right to me. There was something missing, but I didn't know what it was. Something wasn't right. I was confused about the principle of forgiveness as well.

Questions for the Reader:

1. What was I confused about?
2. What led to my confusion?
3. Can you relate to being confused about how someone has mistreated you? If so, write down what happened to you that led to confusion.

CHAPTER 2

SEARCHING

"Wisdom is radiant and unfading, and she is
easily discerned by those who love her, and is
found by those who seek her."

—Wisdom 6:12

Changes

*This is it! I know this will change me. This will take care of
all of my problems! This will make me happy!*

This is what I thought when I accepted my first teaching
position at John Adams Junior High in South Central
Los Angeles. These were the thoughts that came to mind
the first day I walked through the long hallways of the old
inner-city junior high school. I had been preparing for this
experience for a while, and I was excited and ready for it.
Most importantly, I was ready for the incredible changes it
would make in my life. After all, I had chosen to teach in an
inner-city school even when some family members suggested
I teach somewhere else. I would be helping the poor and
disadvantaged. I was placing myself in a difficult position.
I was out of my comfort zone, I was excited, and I truly
believed it would change me.

I spent a total of four years teaching at this school, and it
was a great experience for me. I grew up there as a teacher, and
I was able to be a counselor as well. However, after these four

years, the excitement wore off. I realized I was still the same person with the same problems, and the experience hadn't lived up to my expectations. I had thought the experience would change me for the better, but I hadn't changed.

I was still confused about love and forgiveness—as well as what exactly my father owed me. I thought this experience would make the confusion go away, but it didn't. My relationship with my father wasn't any better. I was unhappy. I made another decision to change my life. I believed going back to school to get a master's degree would solve my internal struggles so I would finally be happy.

I entered my first year at Cal State Northridge studying public health with the same excitement and expectations I had with my first teaching position. My goal was to train myself in this program to manage health programs in third-world countries. No one in my family had earned a college degree—let alone an advanced degree. I would be the first one, and I expected it to change me.

The program was great, but halfway through, I realized I was in the wrong emphasis. I loved epidemiology, the study of disease occurrence, and I should have switched to that emphasis. If I did, it would take longer to finish the degree. I decided to remain within the community health education emphasis and graduate on time. I would have the advanced degree in my hands and experience change in my life.

I finished my master's project, which took a year to complete, and received my degree after three years. However, to my surprise, nothing changed. I didn't feel any different. All I felt was relief that my schooling was over. I expected the degree to change me, but it didn't. I still had the same confusion about love, forgiveness, and what my father owed me. I had suspected that it would make me happy, but it didn't. I thought it would take away my confusion. What had happened? What went wrong? If that didn't change me, what would? What should I do next?

After completing my master's degree, I went back into teaching. I would have my summers off, and I decided to start traveling during my summer vacations. I thought travel would make me worldly and wise. It would change me. It would free me from my confusion and unhappiness. I was sure of it!

My first trip was to the Philippines. I saw third-world poverty and experienced a new culture for the first time. I went to Spain, England, Austria, France, and Switzerland. I went to Israel twice, and I studied Spanish in Guatemala and Costa Rica. I had great experiences and met some great people. However, over time, I grew bored and tired of traveling. The excitement of travel was gone. I realized that my expectations didn't match the reality. My belief in what it would give me didn't come to fruition. I wasn't changed. I continued to ask the same question: What should I do next?

Therapy! That is what I will do next. Someone will challenge me, and I will grow and mature and fix all my problems. I entered therapy with all the previous expectations and excitement for change. After a year of therapy, I grew tired of analyzing my feelings. I grew tired of feeling every emotion in every situation. I stopped after a year. However, I'm glad I did it. It was a step in the right direction for me. It started me on the right track of discovering what my problems were.

In one session, I was complaining to my therapist about all that was wrong with the world. I described my disgust at institutions such as our government and the church.

"Usually when someone is so upset at external institutions, it means they have a problem with an authority figure," my therapist said.

This statement silenced me, and I instantly shut up and stopped complaining.

Is this guy crazy? Obviously there's a lot wrong with our government and with the church today. What kind of nonsense is he talking about? This is what I pay him to come up with? However, could he possibly be right?

I wasn't ready to answer the question at the time. When I left therapy, I grew frustrated and weary about my decisions because nothing was working! Nothing gave me the change and happiness I was looking for. I experienced momentary happiness, which was only momentary excitement. I didn't know what to do next. I was out of ideas, and I was in despair.

Forgive Me for Hating You

"I hated my father for leaving me, and I hated my mother for the way she mistreated me," said Jesse Peterson, a guest on the Dennis Prager's radio show.

That's interesting. I hate my father also. I guess we have something in common, but I can't believe he's admitting such a terrible thing on live radio. I wonder what else he has to say.

"It was through silence that I came to realize what the source of my problems was, and I realized the hate I had for my mother and father was that source. I then had to do something about it. I went to my mom and I asked her to forgive me for hating her for the way she mistreated me," said Jesse Peterson.

When I heard this statement, I sat up straight. Mr. Peterson had the wisdom and understanding that I needed. He had my undivided, focused attention. I was intrigued by what he said. I noticed that he asked his mother to forgive him for hating her. He didn't say that he had forgiven her for mistreating him. This specific point caught my attention because I had always been confused about forgiveness. I didn't understand why I should forgive someone who wronged me if the other person hadn't asked for forgiveness first. I never said it even though my religion taught me to forgive.

The guest admitted that he hated his father and his mother. I made the commitment to hate my father and his mistress with every ounce of emotion, but I never openly admitted it to anyone. I didn't want to show that I was filled with hate, so I hid it. After all, I was a nice guy. I worked with the poor, and I was educated and well traveled. I didn't think anyone would suspect that I was filled with hate.

This guy had my attention, and I had to meet him. There was something about what he said that gripped me and wouldn't let go. I wanted to find out more about him and his beliefs. When he agreed to meet with me, I was excited and nervous.

"Tell me about your life before you asked your mother for forgiveness," I said.

"I lived off the government. I didn't work, and I was on drugs. Eventually, I grew tired of living that way. Also, I had the most difficult time speaking the truth to people."

"What has your life been like since you asked your mother for forgiveness?"

"It has been completely different. I started my own cleaning business, and the business grew. I went back to school. I got off drugs, and I stopped living off the government. I created my own organization called Brotherhood of a New Destiny, and I am now an author of two books. My life has completely changed since asking my mother to forgive me. Most importantly, I now live by the truth. I love the truth, and I love telling the truth."

I was impressed by what he had to say. He had accomplished so much and had changed so much since asking for forgiveness. I admired him for his accomplishments and for picking himself up from such a low place in his life. He seemed to be happy and fulfilled. His life was filled with purpose, and he loved to tell the truth! He possessed characteristics—peace, happiness, and fulfillment—that I wanted. He had a life I desired.

Live by the truth, love the truth, and love telling the truth. These words stuck to me; they pierced my exterior. I kept thinking about them as if they were a mantra. I couldn't get them out of my mind. Why did those words captivate me so much?

"What about your anger? What have you done with it?" Jesse asked during another visit.

I was taken aback. *Was I showing anger? Could he tell I had anger? I don't have anger. I'm a nice guy, and look at all the great things I'm doing with my life.*

"I don't know. I don't know if I have a lot of anger," I replied.

I left his office with more haunting questions. *Am I angry? What have I done with everything that has happened? Have I accepted all those trite and comfortable sayings as the whole truth? Am I covering up my anger? Am I admitting the whole truth about my family situation? Am I admitting the truth about myself and my problems?*

I was captivated by his use of forgiveness. His way of forgiving made sense to me since he took full responsibility for what he allowed to enter him, which was his hatred for his parents. This type of forgiveness seemed to be wise, and I started to believe in it. I stopped being confused about forgiveness.

Questions for the Reader:

1. How did I search for relief from my confusion? Did it work?
2. What captivated me about the way Mr. Peterson forgave his parents?
3. Have you ever searched for a new belief when your present belief didn't make sense to you? If so, write about it.

CHAPTER 3

ACT

"We are divorcing," my sibling said. We were having a family dinner at a restaurant when my sibling told us this. It was my siblings, me, my mother, and my nieces and nephews. Another divorce in our family!

"We had so many problems, but we still love each other," proclaimed this sibling. The sibling listed what the problems were, and then I wondered if those were the problems, how could there have been love within the relationship? It didn't make sense to me, and something sounded so very familiar. Everything got quiet for me. There was talking and arguing going on, but I became very still, quiet, and focused.

Where had I heard this statement before? It sounded so familiar. My mind was racing. I blocked out all the external noise and focused on this one comment. The comment started with describing a relationship as bad and difficult, but ending with "we love each other." The relationship and the spouse were described in negative terms, but they still loved each other. *This sounds so familiar. Where have I heard this statement before?*

"Dad, tell me what your new girlfriend is like," I asked my father.

"She doesn't have many friends, she's married with four children, and she has a temper, but I love her!"

There it was. I found it. That type of statement had been uttered by my father twenty years earlier. It was as if he was saying the same thing at this moment in the restaurant. I became very quiet, and I listened to the other people at the table. I didn't add anything to the conversation because I thought I was on the verge of discovering the truth, and I didn't want the moment to go away.

So what is the truth? What is the connection between the two similar statements? Even though there was chaos at the table, the truth came to me. This belief in love had been learned and was passed on from my father to my sibling. The characteristics of love were negative instead of positive. The belief was that love existed with negativity, shallow emotion, passion, destruction, anger, fear, and hate.

This belief in love is sick. This is the root of so many of my family's problems. This is our problem, and it's why there has been so much destruction in our relationships. This isn't just other people's problems—it is mine as well. I accepted this belief, and I believed this was love. That was why I decided I never wanted it!

I left the restaurant that evening in silence and thinking about the truth I had discovered. *I want to get away from myself. I'm so uncomfortable with myself now.* I started to drive really fast because I wanted to get away from myself. I didn't want to be myself. I didn't want this cancerous belief within me. I realized that my thinking was crazy, and I stopped driving fast since that clearly would not take me away from myself. I knew I had to face myself, but how? The truth was directly and clearly in front of me, but what would I do with it? How could I heal? I had to take full responsibility for what I allowed to be created inside of me—just as Jesse Peterson did.

How do I do this? What do I do? What do I want? What type of person do I want to be? Do I want to hide from the truth or live from the truth? I was filled with anger and hate. I had to finally admit it to myself. I had committed myself to hating my father and his mistress. *How do I rid myself of this commitment? Do I want to be happy and fulfilled like Jesse Peterson? If so, what do I have to do?*

I realized what I had to do once I admitted to myself that I was a hate-filled person and that I had committed myself to hate. I was ready to take full responsibility for my actions based upon this truth.

> Dad, I'm sending you this e-mail because I want to apologize. I want to apologize to you for disrespecting you. Now, all I ask of you is three things: encourage me to be a good person; encourage me to take full responsibility for my actions; and encourage me to do better than you and Mom did.

> Geoff

I pressed send and immediately felt as if a huge weight had been lifted from my shoulders. All I had to do was wait for his reply. *I wonder if he will reply. What will he say? Will he think I'm crazy? I'll just have to wait and see.*

"Hello," I said.

"Hi, Geoff, this is Dad."

What would I say? I started breathing quickly. I told myself to breathe slowly and relax.

"How are you?"

"I'm fine. I read your e-mail, and I tried to write you a letter over the past several weeks, but I couldn't. I decided to call. First, thank you for your e-mail; it really meant a lot to me."

"You're welcome, and I apologize for disrespecting you."

"You have nothing to apologize for."

I thought that it was an out for me. I could take his lead and go back on my apology, but I wouldn't be living the truth.

"No, I disrespected you, and for that I apologize. This was my fault," I said.

"Well, thank you. Geoff, do you want to talk about the divorce?"

"No. I've spent too much time over the past two decades dwelling on that, and I want to move forward."

"Okay. Well, I guess it's onward and upward."

"I agree."

"Good-bye."

"Bye."

Wow! I'm glad that is over. I feel like a thousand-pound weight has been lifted from my shoulders. I did it! I apologized for what I did wrong in our relationship! I'm glad that's over. I'm done with this forgiveness thing. This was a great experience, but I think I'm through with it now. I am happy and relieved I did this. I've reconciled with my dad, and I'm done!

Over the next several months, I observed the three things I had asked of my father were not happening—and he was still very distant. He was stuck in his guilt, and the only thing that would relieve him of his guilt and push him forward was the truth. I decided to have an open, frank conversation with him, but this time in person. I set up a time to meet with him at a restaurant.

"Hey, Dad. How are you?"

"Hi, Geoff. What is it that you need from me?"

"This has nothing to do with me, but it has to do with you. I've noticed over the past couple of months that you are still distant from your children, including me. I've noticed that you haven't tried to reach out to me and offer me the three things I asked of you in my e-mail. It seems to me that you are still consumed with guilt."

"I do feel guilty, and I want to feel guilty, and I should feel guilty for what I did," he said.

"Your guilt should propel you to do the right thing and to reconcile your relationships with your kids."

Only the truth will sent him free. Move forward in the conversation. Get to the truth.

"Dad, you knew I hated you for your affair?"

"Yes, I knew," he said with his head bowed.

"This is what I apologize for. In my e-mail and on the phone, I said I apologized for disrespecting you. I didn't have the courage at the time to say the truth, but now I do. Now I apologize for hating you for your affair. I realized the hate inside of me for you did me absolutely no good. I have a question to ask you."

"Go ahead."

"Why did you hate us?"

His face turned red, and he was taken aback. "Well, Geoff, *hate* is such a strong word. I wouldn't say I hated you, but …"

He started to ramble. I told myself to stay calm and allow him some time to ramble, but eventually I had to come back to the same question. I had to come back to the truth.

"Dad, if you didn't hate us, certain things wouldn't have happened, like you allowing your alcoholic mistress to call our house and harass us. I'm going to ask the same question again—why did you hate us?"

He seemed more receptive this time. He went into deep thought, and he was struggling to answer the question. He was moving uncomfortably in his chair. His head was lowered, he started to turn red, and his breathing started to labor.

I told myself to remain calm and give him time to answer the question.

"I guess, I guess it was because …"

And, for the first time in decades, my dad told the truth. He finally told the truth! It isn't my place to write what his truth was because it's his to tell, but I will say that his hate stemmed from our family system.

He finally told the truth. I can't believe it! He finally, after twenty years, told the truth! And he started to speak freely.

"I knew what I did was wrong. All along I knew my affair was wrong. I knew it harmed you children. I knew my affair negatively affected you and your siblings. I was wrong. This was the biggest mistake of my life."

After all these years, I'm hearing the truth. I've thought I was crazy all these years, but now I know I wasn't crazy for being confused by his affair.

The unadulterated truth was that his affair was wrong. He admitted it with no excuses. The truth was before him, and it was his choice to decide what he wanted to do with it. I wondered what he was going to do.

"Dad, I want to thank you for telling the truth. I really appreciate it. I know it was hard for you, but now your truth is out in the open. It is now yours to deal with as you see fit," I said as we were leaving the restaurant.

The next time I saw my dad was at a family function.

"Well, Geoff, I did it. I actually did it," he said.

"What did you do?"

"I wrote a letter to your mother to apologize for the way I mistreated her and our children."

"You did? Dad, that's great. I know that took a lot of courage. I'm very proud of you."

"Thanks, but I haven't heard back from her. I'm feeling uneasy because I don't know what she thinks."

"Dad, you took full responsibility for your actions by apologizing to her. Her response is up to her and not up to you."

I can't believe he did this! He took full responsibility for his terrible, destructive behavior and said the truth to my mom. I love that he used the word mistreated because that is exactly what he did, and he didn't offer any excuses. I never expected all of this to happen. I never expected this kind of movement from asking for forgiveness. It went from me to my dad and then to my mom. This is unbelievable! I wonder if there is more to reconciling this relationship.

Questions for the Reader:

1. Describe the type of forgiveness Jesse Peterson applied in his life.
2. Why did this type of forgiveness captivate me?
3. What is your belief in forgiveness? What does it look like?

CHAPTER 4

RECONCILE

Death Happens and So Do Miracles

Trust was reborn in my relationship with my father, and I could finally answer the question of what my father owed me. He owed me the truth, and he gave it to me.

What did I owe him? I owed him time. I called him up and asked to get together. I wanted to listen to him. He liked to talk about history, politics, and religion. I engaged him and listened to him. I had never done that before. I enjoyed those times, especially since he stopped saying anything negative about my mother. I also realized another thing I owed him: I had to take care of him since he was getting older.

He became jaundiced. His skin was yellow. When I saw him for the first time, I was shocked. The four siblings took him to the doctor, and the doctor discovered he had cancer again. The cancer was operable and didn't require radiation or chemotherapy.

Two of my dad's wishes came true. He never wanted to go through those two things—and he never had to. The four-hour surgery went well; in a week, he was able to leave the hospital and go to my sister's house for recovery. He was slowly regaining his strength, but he was very thin. He only weighed 105 pounds. Eventually, he was strong enough to return to his house and live on his own, which he wanted to do.

We all drove down to his sister's house in San Clemente for Father's Day. We spent about six hours together and enjoyed each other's company. I am truly amazed that I had begun to enjoy his company.

It turned out to be the last time I saw him. He suddenly passed away from a heart attack in his house on June 28, 2006. Below is a copy of the speech I gave at his memorial service; it summarizes how we reconciled. I found there was still more to the process of reconciling a broken relationship. No words have been changed.

Miracles

I want to speak to everyone today about miracles. Miracles are those unexpected, joyous occurrences in life that happen when two people take risks to reconcile a broken relationship. The two people I'm going to be speaking about are me and my father, James Leroy Woods Jr. I believe these miracles will honor and celebrate my father because you will know what type of man he became, and I hope these miracles will inspire you. So, please, listen carefully. The first miracle I want to talk about is the miracle of truth.

The Miracle of Truth

Truth is so miraculous because it gives human beings absolute clarity to what their problems are. So many people in life let disappointment turn into anger, then bitterness, and then over time it turns into hate. This is exactly what I did with my father; I was very disappointed in his words and actions, and over time I allowed this disappointment to turn into hate. I am ashamed to say that I hated my father. Let me be clear: my problem wasn't the way my father treated me—my real problem was I allowed hate to enter and live within me. Once I realized my truth, I wanted desperately to get rid of this ugliness. The miracle of my truth led me to the miracle of forgiveness.

The Miracle of Forgiveness

Forgiveness allows human beings to try to make right out of what they have done wrong. This is exactly what I wanted to do with my father. Over two conversations with my father, I asked my father to forgive me for hating him, and I asked him to do three things: to encourage me to take full responsibility for my choices; to encourage me to do better than he and my mother; and to encourage me to be a good person. Before forgiveness, I knew he felt guilty, and I manipulated him to get what I wanted. On the other side of forgiveness, I only wanted encouragement from him. I started the process with him in trying to make right out of what I did wrong. This miracle led to the miracle of compassion and courage.

The Miracle of Compassion and Courage

In my opinion, compassion is not feeling sorry for someone, but it's about wanting people to heal, and it often takes the miracle of courage to help a person heal. Asking the right question is the courageous act that allows someone to start the healing process. This question is often difficult to ask, and it is very, very difficult to answer.

Several months had passed since I apologized to my father, and I noticed he hadn't encouraged me to do anything of the three things I requested. I only knew too well how hate can control a person, and I knew what was within me was in him, and I wanted him to heal. I set up a time to meet with him, and I knew the right question to ask him to release his guilt. When I met with him, I told him this meeting has nothing to do with me, but everything to do with him. I continued to say that I saw him distant from his children and that he seemed to be stuck in his guilt; I added that I wanted him to heal.

I finally had the courage to ask him the right question. I asked, "Why did you hate us?" As you can imagine, he was shocked. He told me that this question seemed extreme, and I said I know. But the great thing about my father that night was he didn't avoid the question; he struggled to answer it. I watched him squirm and turn a little pale.

He said, "Geoff, this is really difficult."

And I said, "Dad, I know."

And finally, he answered the question, and there was his truth that had been buried for so many decades. I didn't judge his truth, but I accepted it. And now he was free; he was free to choose to act upon his truth. Let me tell you exactly what my dad did with his truth.

When I saw him the next time, he said, "Geoff, I did it."

I said, "Dad, what did you do?"

He said, "I wrote to your mother, and I apologized to her for mistreating her and our children."

I said, "Dad, I'm very proud of you. I know that was difficult and took a lot of courage."

This, to me, was a miracle. And it is this act of forgiveness that keeps coming to my mind as I've been thinking about my dad since he passed away. And I want all of you to remember this very rare act by my father. How many human beings have the courage to face their truth, and then try to make right out of what they have done wrong? My dad was one of the few who had the courage to do this. At this moment, he became a great man to me because I believe men are created to tell the truth. I could now trust him, and love him, and start a new relationship with him, and he, in turn, could do the same with me.

I believe the highest honor you can give someone is emulation; I encourage you to emulate my father. My father experienced the miracle of truth followed by the miracle of forgiveness. These miracles led to the miracle of kind gestures.

The Miracle of Kind Gestures

It is the very act of kind gestures that renews, grows, and matures a broken relationship. Let me tell you what my dad did next. He gave me a Christmas card, and inside it he wrote that I was a blessing to him. This was the greatest gift I had ever received from him; I accepted this as true because

I believed I had been a blessing to him. And, after all these years, I finally felt like my father's son.

This kind gesture deserved another kind gesture in return. So I called him up and asked to get together with him, and when we met, all we did was talk and listen to each other. There was no pointing of fingers and no blame.

His kind gesture showed me that I needed to thank him for something I had neglected to do for many years. When I was a young boy, my father had stomach cancer surgery, and his recuperation process was very, very difficult. I watched him get up every morning and go to work despite his health difficulties. I told my dad I was very grateful for this act; he told me he appreciated my gratitude. Kind gestures can really renew a broken relationship. This miracle led to the miracle of healing.

The Miracle of Healing

True healing occurs when you desire the very person that hurt you to heal, and this is why healing is an incredible miracle. This past March, my dad had another cancer surgery, and the surgery was successful.

After his surgery, some friends and I went to his condo to pray for him. We gathered around him and placed our hands on him. I remember placing my left hand on his very slight right shoulder, and I thought to myself that I am now praying for healing for a man whom I used to be so angry with. However, I didn't feel any anger or hatred toward him at all; these feelings were gone.

And, please hear this, these feelings were a big waste of my time since nothing good came from them. This was a God-given miracle. And as we continued to pray, I heard my dad crying, and when he had a chance to speak, he said this was one of the best experiences of his life. What I know to be true is that hate is very powerful, but love based upon the truth, forgiveness, and healing is way more powerful. This was a profound moment of healing for both of us. I next want to speak about the miracle of facing the fear of death.

The Miracle of Facing the Fear of Death

Since my father had his first cancer surgery over thirty years ago, I have been afraid that he was going to die, and because of this, I distanced myself from him. Little did I know I would come face-to-face with his death on Wednesday, June 28. My youngest sister, Mary, and I went to his condo to check on him; he had been sick that day and hadn't answered his phone. I expected to find him asleep, but as we entered his condo and I peered around the corner into his bedroom, I saw he had fallen on the foot of his bed. He looked so lonely and frail, and I went into shock. I yelled out, "Dad!" and went running toward him. I shook him to see if he was actually asleep, but his eyes didn't open. I ran back to my sister and told her to call 911, and then I ran back to him. I shook him again to try to wake him up; I checked for a pulse, but there was none. I realized then that he was dead. And, with tears in my eyes, I then ran to my sister and asked her if she knew his street number, and she said no. I ran outside to get his street number, and then I ran back to him. I noticed this time that he was naked, and the last thing I did for my father was to cover his nakedness.

This, to me, was a real miracle. How was it that I was able to keep running toward my dad in his death since I had been so afraid of this for many decades? Many people have helped me to gain insight to this miracle. I think I was able to do this because I moved forward toward him in life, which gave me the strength to do this in his death. I believe God gave me the strength to do this from all the previous miracles that had occurred between me and my father.

I believe my sister and I were there to perform one last act of service for my father, and that act of service was to care for his body. My sister took care of all of the administrative things, such as calling 911 and calling the mortuary. She lived in that moment out of her strength and giftedness, and she did it beautifully. This was her last act of service for my father, and my last act of service for him was to cover his nakedness.

Even though this was very difficult for me, and continues to be, it was really an honor and a privilege to do this for our father. My brother, Craig, and my sisters, Carol and Mary, have been very concerned about me. They gave me wise advice, and for once, I followed it. In turn, I want to say to the three of you, I am glad I found Dad so that you didn't have to. You are now free to heal yourselves and your families. Please accept this as a loving and benevolent gift from God. God strengthened me to do this, and I know God will give me the strength and wisdom to heal. I thank the three of you very much for your concern. This was truly a miracle, which led to the next miracle of peace.

The Miracle of Peace

To have peace among shock and trauma is truly a miracle. This is a peace that surpasses all understanding, and it is a direct gift from God. Even though it was shocking to find my dad, I have peace. I was at peace with our relationship before he died, and I am at peace with our relationship in his death. This peace came from both of us reconciling with each other; this peace took work to achieve. I am also at peace with the way he died. He didn't die of cancer, which is a miracle. He didn't have to do chemotherapy or radiation; he wasn't in a hospital. He died at his house, and he lived independently up until his last breath. I believe he died quickly and without pain. It was a blessing to him and a blessing to his children that he didn't suffer. I am at peace. This leads to the next miracle, which is the miracle of faith in God.

The Miracle of Faith in God

The purpose of faith in God is transformation. Faith has the ability to transform human beings from the inside out—to move them from bitterness, anger, resentment, and hate into truth, forgiveness, reconciliation, healing, and peace. Truth, forgiveness, reconciliation, healing, and peace are all tenets of my Christian faith. I believe it was the prompting of God's Holy Spirit that led me and my dad to reconcile. And to experience all these miracles, all I had to do was submit and obey the tenets of my faith. I know for myself, I would not have done these acts of my own volition. And whom do I have to thank for introducing me to faith in God? I thank my parents, Alice Parker, my mother, and especially my father, James Leroy Woods Jr. My dad was a man of great faith. I give all thanks to my earthly father as well as my heavenly Father.

I thank God for being my creator who wants to recreate me. I thank him for sending his son, Jesus Christ, who is my savior, and who was a great example of a man who told the truth. I believe he actually died because he told the truth. And I am so very grateful for God's profound love for me. I know God loves me because he requires me to be more than my anger, more than my bitterness, and more than my hatred. Thanks be to God! This leads me to talk about the last miracle—the miracle of gratitude.

The Miracle of Gratitude

Offering people thanks for their kindness is at the least acknowledging and encouraging kind gestures, and at the most is acknowledging and encouraging people's experiences, wisdom, and giftedness. It is a very important act. There have been so many people who have helped me and my family through this difficult ordeal. I appreciate your words of wisdom, your phone calls, your e-mails, your prayers, your presence, and your help. They have truly been a blessing to me and my family.

I really want to thank everyone who is here today. I know this isn't a very comfortable situation, but your presence is greatly appreciated, and I am so humbled by it. Your kind, thoughtful gesture deserves another kind gesture. I offer to all of you who are here the miracles and lessons I have described to you today. I humbly and freely give them as gifts to you. Accept them, use them wisely, and use them often. I again encourage you to honor my father by emulating the incredible miracles that he did in his life.

I hope these miracles have inspired you to believe differently, to love differently, and to use your faith differently. I hope they have raised important questions in your minds, such as have you faced the reality of death so you can freely live? Are you at peace with your past and present relationships? Are you living with hope or are you living out of despair? Are you willing to experience the miracle of truth and forgiveness like my father?

I encourage you to take these miracles and make them your own. I also want to encourage you to share your miracles with others; you never know who might need them for inspiration. I thank you very much for listening to me, and I thank you very much for your presence here today. Thank you.

Miracles. I can't believe all of these miracles happened. I never expected all of them to occur. I couldn't have written what would happen. I learned so many different lessons. You retard your growth as a person if you don't face the truth of what you have allowed to be created inside of you. You also allow someone else to retard their growth if you don't confront them on how they have wronged you.

I realized forgiveness doesn't have to do with only me, but also my father. Forgiveness isn't singular; it is plural. I often hear people say if you don't forgive, you are hurting yourself, which is true but not the whole truth. The other person is hurting as well, and only the truth will set the person free. Asking for forgiveness allows you to believe differently, act differently, and love differently—and what I mean by differently is better, deeper, and more meaningful.

I do believe in love now, but it isn't the same kind of love I grew up with and watched and observed. I now believe love has to do with telling the truth; it has to do with coming along beside someone and at the appropriate time telling the truth. The purpose isn't just to make you feel better or do better but to help the person grow and mature into a decent human being.

I had never used my faith in this way. It was my faith in God that led me to do all of this; it was not of myself. I obeyed and stepped out in faith. I am thankful to God that he loves his creation so much that he requires things of us. He requires us to reconcile with each other when we have broken trust in a relationship, and he shows us how. He shows us how through other people.

I'm thankful to have met and spoken with Jesse Peterson. I observed great changes in a man who stepped out in faith and healed himself and those around him. I was able to observe a fellow human being do what was right and observe him putting his faith in action and seeing the results. We are to be humble examples of how to make right out of that which is wrong.

Questions for the Reader:

1. What is my definition of a miracle?
2. What steps did I take to reconcile with my father?
3. Is there anyone in your life you need to reconcile with? How will you go about doing this?

CHAPTER 5

Freedom

The word *freedom* is so rich in meaning, and it's so desirous that people sacrifice their time and energy to obtain it. This is probably true since freedom offers individuals so much hope, and people look for this hope born from freedom in different ways. There is religious freedom, political freedom, and—one I never realized existed until I reconciled with my father—personal freedom. Any type of freedom, including personal freedom, is the liberation from some type of control or power.

Webster's Dictionary describes freedom as "the release from imprisonment and the ability to act and move in a different and profound way." I am defining personal freedom as the freedom from unresolved anger, hatred, and confusion caused by deceit. After many decades of struggle, I found personal freedom from the power and control of emotional hate.

How exactly was I imprisoned? I was imprisoned by my own choice to hate my father and his mistress with every ounce of emotion I had. This type of hate shackled me and had a profound grip on me, and it did not give me the power I thought it would. It had control over me instead of me having control over it, and I let it have control over me for several decades.

How was I liberated from this imprisonment by hate? I was liberated through a new, profound, meaningful belief in forgiveness. I had to search for this meaningful belief in forgiveness, and I had one criterion for accepting the principle of forgiveness, and that was it had to make sense to me. I didn't want to forgive my father and allow his bad behavior and poor choices to go without any type of sound judgment or consequence, and I didn't want to ask forgiveness and take on all the responsibility for what went wrong in our relationship.

The belief in forgiveness I found was one that said I was to take complete responsibility over what I did wrong. I often thought of myself as the victim in the relationship and, therefore, never thought I did anything wrong—and I was wrong! When I found this new belief in forgiveness, I then had to apply it. I apologized to my father for hating him. I took full responsibility for this, and once I did this, the hate no longer had control over me, but I had control over it.

Wisdom's Freedom

When hate no longer had control over me, a space inside me was ready to be filled with something else, and I recognized it had to be filled with something better and greater than emotional hate. I could now start to create a new life based upon beliefs born out of what was true, good, and honest. *True* means it is based upon objective truth, which comes from my faith. *Good* means that it doesn't only have to do with me. And *honest* means it isn't based upon lies. I decided to start with my belief in love.

Remember, I didn't believe in love at all. Looking back with my experience with my father, I was able to create a new belief in love. I now strongly believe in love, but I don't believe love is based upon empty, shallow emotions or feelings, and I don't believe love is negative or destructive. I believe love is deeper and more profound than that.

I now know love to be the act of coming alongside someone and telling him or her the truth at an appropriate time. The sole purpose of telling the truth to the person is so the person will heal, and, hopefully, out of this healing process, the person will do what is right.

Recall that wisdom teaches people to engage in good conduct. The way to possess good conduct is to find beliefs that are based upon what is true, good, and honest and then apply these beliefs. This is the rich source of freedom that wisdom offers people.

The Source of Wisdom

I now want to be very clear to my readers about my experience in reconciling with my father. I have written what I have done, but none of this would have been possible without my Christian faith.

The true source of my freedom and wisdom is God. The idea of forgiveness came from my faith. I heard about this principle a lot through church, but I was confused by how I saw people apply it. Oftentimes, it takes viewing how another human being has applied a faith principle to fully comprehend it, believe it, and then act upon it.

God led me to search for a belief in forgiveness that made sense to me, he led me to Jesse Peterson, and he gave me the idea to apologize to my father for hating him and then confront my father on why he hated his family. I believe the idea came to me from God because this idea was the furthest thing from my mind. I had never thought of doing this, and on an emotional level, I didn't want to do it.

I didn't want to confront him, but I knew I had to do it. If I didn't do it, I would be disobeying God, and I didn't want to do that. When I finally used my faith correctly, it led to miracles. I never expected any of this to happen. Wisdom given by God and obeyed by humans starts with new beliefs in faith principles that lead to acts of courage that lead to reconciled relationships, which are the very fruits of wisdom.

I also found something that was worth more than any material possession on earth. I really found true treasure and value in wisdom from God. If someone were to say to me that he would give me $5 million and take away all the hurt, confusion, pain, and fear, I would say no. What I experienced was more valuable than fame or fortune. It has become a great value and asset in my life. I now have a firm foundation on which to live—one where I am not manipulated emotionally, and I can stand firm when life and its challenges become difficult. This foundation is reliable and a great source of strength since it comes from God and not myself.

I have truly found gold!

Questions for the Reader:

1. What type of freedom did I find?
2. What was the source of my freedom?
3. What are the steps to acquiring wisdom?
4. What are the fruits of wisdom?
5. Do you think wisdom from God is a source of happiness?